# Every Body

*The Anointing of Discipline*

## C V Lewis

## YANA Ministries

Publisher Yana Ministries

Year 2017

First Printing: 2017

ISBN 978-0-9935986-2-3
978-0-9935986-3-0

Published by YANA Ministries
SE6, London, England
United Kingdom
www.yanaministries.wix.com/yana

# Dedication

To my lovely husband and children.

For encouraging and believing in me to accomplish greater dreams than I have ever dreamt.

Thank you best friend.

# Contents

# Acknowledgements

I thank my husband, Ray Lewis, without whose help this book would never have been completed.

I thank my sisters Pastor Pearline Bent and First Lady Claudia Williams-Silvera; your support and prayers as I lived through this book to restore my health and my leisure have been a tower of strength for me.

My heartfelt thanks to those who wrote to me after the release of *Food for Thought* and sent pictures, all with encouragement for me to continue in the call to share God's Word. It was a welcomed surprise, support, and encouragement. It truly is not the quantity but the quality of friends that bless your life.

# Preface

Having a full-time job, a large, young family as well as increasing ministerial duties at church, I became more aware of my physical body.

Over a period of time, I went through several physical challenges ranging from tiredness to full on stress, which affected me negatively.

I sought refuge in the Word of God; I was looking for a scripture or two to keep me going.  But I found so much more. I started to understand I needed to get my physical body back to good health.

For years, I have seen people operate under less than 100% physical or mental efficiency and thought it was acceptable because I was results driven. I thought as long as you get your desired result, then it was worth the sleepless nights and the stress.

However, I found that God has provided a way of escape and in many cases, we have a duty to get our bodies in alignment with the Word of God.  When we don't, our results in the spirit and body are limited or off target.

We gain better results in all aspects of our lives when we are aligned with Gods Word.

I hope by sharing what God has imparted to me, I will help you to grow more in wisdom and knowledge concerning your health.

I aim to get you to use the authority you have in the Spirit through the physical body and the appreciation of care applied to your body by sanctification.

C V Lewis

# Introduction

No matter who we are in the body of Christ, how anointed we are or how long we have been in Christ, we all have something common. Something that does not consider doctrine, teaching practices or messages; it is our bodies.

We all have physical bodies, whatever condition they may be in. Our tendency is to focus on our spiritual bodies; however, in this book, I show you the power that we can only exercise in this physical body, not after we have gone to heaven.

Our physical bodies have a direct link to how we move and operate in the spiritual realm.

I look at the importance of the physical body according to the Word of God and explain in depth its sanctification.

There are 6 major physical areas, which we are told in the Word of God to take care of. You will be amazed how something we regard as insignificant or only for the few is actually a general mandate for all of us to function and operate better in our spirits, souls, and bodies.

Though this book approaches the body from a biblical perspective, the principle in Chapter 4 applies to every human body whether it is in Christ or not.

Christ died for everyone. God's guidance for taking care of the body is not solely for those who choose Him. However, it does have greater ministerial benefits when adhered to by His children.

C V Lewis

## Chapter 1: The Importance of the Human Body

Your physical body is important. It is essential to how you live here on earth, your eternity, spiritual power and your authority. They all operate in it.

The church today often separates the importance of the physical body, which houses the spiritual being. The focus is usually on the spiritual body and the eternal, immortal bodies we will all receive.

Usually, when the church talks about the physical body, it surrounds the topic of physical healing and deliverance.

However, the very spiritual authority that we walk in is dependent upon our bodies. It is the seat of our authority given by God way back in the garden of Eden. Your body is also needed to house your God-given power. In fact, the body is a prime location.

### **We are Spirits who Live in Bodies**

The New Testament teaches that our spirituality cannot be separated from the physical. The apostle Paul wrote:

*"What? Do you not know that your body is the temple of the Holy Spirit, who is in you, whom you have received from God, and that you are not your own?"*

*(1 Corinthians 6:19).*

Your body is desired real estate.  It is needed for you to operate here on the earth.  God's Spirit longs to dwell within it and the Devil would also like to possess it.

Do not overlook the importance of your body; it's the base of your legal authority. You read correctly; your body has been given the right or legal authority to rule here on the earth.

Yes, you are a spirit housed in a body, but it is that body, which activates the authority.

> *Then the LORD God formed the man of dust from the ground and breathed into his nostrils the breath of life, and the man became a living creature (Genesis 2:7).*

In Genesis, we are told that we became living creatures when we were clothed with the dust of the ground. God breathed life into the body, but He did not stop there.

> *Then God said, "Let us make man in our image, after our likeness. And let them have dominion over the fish of the sea and over the birds of the heavens and over the livestock and over all the earth and over every creeping thing that creeps on the earth"*
> *(Genesis 1:26).*

It is after the body is made that God gives us the authority to rule through it.  It is a combination of the spirit and body that gives the authority.

Your spirit by itself without the body is an unlawful or illegal authority. When the body dies, you cannot remain or hang around.  You cannot experience authority in your spirit alone. This is why demons and paranormal activities are not lawful on the earth.

Even demons know the importance of a physical body in order to function.

> *For as the body apart from the spirit is dead*
> *(James 2:26).*

As a spiritual being, when the body dies, the earthly authority held within it goes also. This is why God needs us to act now, to walk in our authority now.

## The Difference between Lawful and Unlawful Authority

Satan has no authority; he is an angel and authority was not given to angels or spirits. In order for Satan to gain the authority given to man, he needed to obtain it lawfully by being clothed with a willing body, which holds the authority.

We know that God walked and talked with Adam and Eve in the garden of Eden, but many people ask why God did not take over and intervene there and put an end to Satan's plan.

God had the power to put an end to Satan's plan, but God is not made of flesh or housed in a body. Therefore, He did not have the earthly authority.  God will not go against His law. If He does, He will be going against His Word. Dirt man has the authority; God has the power.

 Power and authority are often used interchangeably; there is a clear distinction. Jesus clearly describes the difference and the importance of each in John Chapter 5 when He had healed someone and was questioned by what power He did it. Jesus explained that as the Son of God, He has the power given to Him by God:

> *And I assure you that the time is coming, indeed it's*
> *here now, when the dead will hear my voice--the voice*
> *of the Son of God. And those who listen will live. For as*

> *the Father hath life in himself; and he has granted*
> *that same life-giving power to his Son*
> *(John 5:25-26 NLT).*

Further, He explained that as the Son of Man, He has the authority to release that power.

> *And hath given him authority to execute judgment*
> *also, because he is the Son of man*
> *(John 5:27).*

Jesus, being Son of God = Power

Jesus, being Son of Man = Authority

The distinction of being man (a dirt body) is very important in these verses.

There is never any question as to God's power or the power that we have within us given by the indwelling of the Holy Spirit.

> *Beloved, now are we the sons of God*
> *(1 John 3:2).*

> *He predestined us for adoption as sons through Jesus*
> *Christ, according to the purpose of his will.*
> *(Ephesians 1:5).*

We have been adopted as sons of God, which entitles us to move in this power.

When God destroyed Sodom and Gomorrah, He had the power to do so. However, He did not go it alone; He spoke with a man who held earthly authority.

The authority or agreement was from Abraham; God was not acting alone.

The miracles God did for the children of Israel in the wilderness were all by His power. Nevertheless, in each case, He had the authority or agreement of Moses and Aaron. There is always a man for the plan of God.

God will not move without our authority, and we cannot move without God's power. Likewise, demons need to inhabit a dirt body to gain your authority. There is a fight for your body; they all want in.

> *When the unclean spirit is gone out of a man, he*
> *walketh through dry places, seeking rest*
> *(Matthew 12:43).*

Do not underestimate your physical body! Nothing in the spiritual or angelic realm does.

## The Authority

The authority you carry can change your world. It is there to release the power God has placed within you.

*Behold, I have given you authority to tread on serpents and scorpions, and over all the power of the enemy, and nothing shall hurt you*

*(Luke 10:19).*

*But that you may know that the Son of Man has authority on earth to forgive sins—he said to the man who was paralyzed—"I say to you, rise, pick up your bed and go home"*
*(Luke 5:24).*

You have authority to change things in the kingdom of heaven.

*I will give you the keys of the kingdom of heaven, and whatever you bind on earth shall be bound in heaven, and whatever you loose on earth shall be loosed in heaven*
*(Matthew 16:15-19).*

The authority we have in our bodies even gives us the power to remove demons and repair the physical body to health.

> *And he called the twelve together and gave them*
> *power and authority over all demons and to cure*
> *diseases*
> *(Luke 9:1).*

This spiritual authority is given to using the power we have to change things in this world and also in the spiritual realm.

> *For though we walk in the flesh, we are not waging*
> *war according to the flesh. For the weapons of our*
> *warfare are not of the flesh but have divine power to*
> *destroy strongholds. We destroy arguments and every*
> *lofty opinion raised against the knowledge of God and*
> *take every thought captive to obey Christ*
> *(2 Corinthians 10:3-5).*

Our fight is not with the body. The authority the body gives us allows us to overcome in the spiritual realm.

> *For we do not wrestle against flesh and blood, but*
> *against the rulers, against the authorities, against the*
> *cosmic powers over this present darkness, against the*
> *spiritual forces of evil in the heavenly places*
> *(Ephesians 6:12).*

All of the authority we operate and fight in is done through our mortal bodies. We cannot fight without it! Therefore, we should treat our bodies right, giving them the care and attention needed. Your body is the seat of your authority to rule and change your world.

You long for an immortal body free from sickness and pain, but don't disregard the important biblical principles about the mortal body  God has fashioned for you.

# Chapter 2: Sanctify the Body

Your body is not just here to house your spirit and operate in authority; it is a vital part of your worship.

> *I beseech you therefore, brethren, by the mercies of God, that ye present your bodies a living sacrifice, holy, acceptable unto God, which is your reasonable service*
> *(Romans 12:1).*

The above passage focuses on the presentation of our human bodies (made from dirt) to God, which is our reasonable service.

There is a tendency these days to focus on the condition of our hearts and ensuring it is acceptable before the Lord during worship. But there is a requirement to get the body right as well:

> *Now may the God of peace himself sanctify you completely, and may your whole spirit and soul and body be kept blameless at the coming of our Lord Jesus Christ*
> *(1 Thessalonians 5:23).*

We are told to sanctify every part of us—spirits, souls, and our bodies to keep all three blameless at the coming of our Lord.

There are thousands of books and sermons, which discuss the spirit and soul, how to get them right before God and how to change them God-ward. But what about the body? What does it mean to sanctify our bodies? What does it mean to make our bodies holy? How do we present them blameless before the Lord?

The word "sanctify" means to set apart for a particular use set apart as or declare holy; consecrate.

The word "holy" means to dedicate or consecrate to God or a religious purpose.

To sanctify your body is to set it apart from the worldly standards of use and focus on what God requires from our bodies.

*Therefore, if anyone cleanses himself from what is dishonorable, he will be a vessel for honorable use, set apart as holy, useful to the master of the house, ready for every good work*
*(2 Timothy 2:21).*

It is important to know how to cleanse ourselves and what to cleanse ourselves from. Without this knowledge, we will be in danger of embracing or rejecting the wrong things.

*Since we have these promises, beloved, let us cleanse ourselves from every defilement of body and spirit, bringing holiness to completion in the fear of God*
*(2 Corinthians 7:1).*

To sanctify your body, it requires work and focus on your part. Too often, it is assumed that your body is sanctified or made holy when you are saved. This is not the case; we need to present our bodies in an acceptable way. In other words, we need to willingly honour God with our bodies:

*As it is my eager expectation and hope that I will not be at all ashamed, but that with full courage now as always Christ will be honored in my body, whether by life or by death*
*(Philippians 1:20).*

God wants all of you, not just your spirit, not just the transformation of your mind but the dedication of your body to Him. He needs to be honored in your body.

These three: spirit, soul, and body make a consecrated life; they are all your reasonable service.

## Chapter 3: Why Must We Sanctify the Body?

I often hear people refer to the day when they will have new bodies, which will not get sick and that they will not have to worry about their size or shape.

*So we do not lose heart. Though our outer self is wasting away, our inner self is being renewed day by day*
*(2 Corinthians 4:16).*

Although it is great and commendable to remember that there is more and greater to come, you should not do so at the neglect or rejection of your earthly body right now.

You should not be sitting back and "letting nature have its way with your body." This term is often attributed to a person who neglects the care of his or her body and has little or no concern for it.

So the question may be asked, why do we need to place any importance on this physical body?

Taking care of your body is important to God, Jesus, and the Holy Spirit so what's important to them should be important to you.

- ***Made by God***

*Then the LORD God formed the man of dust from the
ground and breathed into his nostrils the breath of
life, and the man became a living creature
(Genesis 2:7).*


*Know that the LORD, he is God! It is he who made us,
and we are his; we are his people, and the sheep of his
pasture
Psalm 100:3).*

We were made and fashioned by God. This is no mistake. God made us on purpose and for His pleasure. No matter how you look at it, God has a design for you. You are not a mistake!

*For you formed my inward parts; you knitted me
together in my mother's womb. I praise you, for I am
fearfully and wonderfully made. Wonderful are your
works; my soul knows it very well. My frame was not
hidden from you, when I was being made in secret,
intricately woven in the depths of the earth. Your eyes
saw my unformed substance
(Psalm 139:13-17).*

Your body was formed with purpose. We are asked to be good stewards over the things God has entrusted into our care.  We have a responsibility to take care of something made by God's own hand and loaned to us for a season of time.

- ***Died for by Christ***

The worth of your body is of such importance to God that He sent His only begotten Son to die for it.

> *He himself bore our sins in his body on the tree, that we might die to sin and live to righteousness. By his wounds you have been healed*
> *(1 Peter 2:24).*

Often times, we hear how Jesus came to save our souls and how our spirits are revived and redeemed, but we must also remember that His sacrifice was for our physical bodies also.

Over one-third of Jesus' ministry was about our physical bodies and our physical health. It is not hidden from scripture that God wants us to be healthy and well. He wants the blind to receive their sight, the lame to walk and the sick to be healed.

Jesus paid for the sicknesses in our physical bodies by being tortured and with His life. For by His stripes, we receive healing to our bodies. What a great price He paid for the body you often overlook and mistreat. Our bodies are of such importance to the Father.

*For God so loved the world, that he gave his only Son, that whoever believes in him should not perish but have eternal life (John3:16).*

*So Jesus also suffered outside the gate in order to sanctify the people through his own blood (Hebrews 13:12).*

*And by that will we have been sanctified through the offering of the body of Jesus Christ once for all (Hebrews 10:10).*

The shedding of His blood and the sacrifice of His life were not just for our eternity but for our growth and well-being right now in the body.

Jesus' blood was shed for our healing in the body, which is a key factor in the well-being of our hearts, minds, and souls.

Our bodies are not our own; they are on loan. A high price was paid for something often ignored by so many.

- ***Lived in by the Holy Spirit***

Your body houses you, and you are a spirit. But you are not a single occupant of your house.

As Christians, we should have dual occupancy of our bodies that are shared with the Holy Spirit.

> *Do you not know that you are God's temple and that God's Spirit dwells in you?*
> *(1 Corinthians 3:16).*

Our bodies are valuable to the Holy Spirit; He lives in them.

Before the sacrifice made by Christ, the presence of the Holy Spirit throughout the Word of God referred to the Spirit coming upon a person to do the work of God. He did not dwell within the body of that person.

> *And it shall come to pass afterward, that I will pour out my Spirit on all flesh*
> *Joel 2:28).*

> *The Spirit of the Lord GOD is upon me*
> *(Isaiah 61:1).*

> *And the Spirit of the LORD shall rest upon him, the Spirit of wisdom and understanding, the Spirit of counsel and might, the Spirit of knowledge and the fear of the LORD*
> *(Isaiah 11:2).*

We can see from the three verses above, which are only a few from the Old Testament, that when the Spirit was mentioned, there was no occupancy of the body.

Now, since Jesus paid the price for our spirits, soul, and bodies, we are the Holy Spirit's temples.

> *Or do you not know that your body is a temple of the*
> *Holy Spirit within you, whom you have from God?*
> *(1 Corinthians 6:19-20).*

The Holy Spirit does more than help our spirits and souls; He helps our physical bodies. Romans 8 tells how, He, the Holy Spirit gives life to our mortal bodies.

> *If the Spirit of him who raised Jesus from the dead*
> *dwells in you, he who raised Christ Jesus from the*
> *dead will also give life to your mortal bodies through*
> *his Spirit who dwells in you*
> *(Romans 8:11).*

We are made by God, bought for by Christ and lived in by the Holy Spirit.

This body, which is sometimes forgotten in this fast-paced environment has never been or will never be forgotten by God as long as you still occupy it.

You are like a china cup made by the best potter, redeemed for an astronomical price and used to serve the best tea within your vessel.

## Chapter 4: How Do We Take Care of the Body

Often times, the condition of our bodies are the result of what we do. People tend to act in the interest of their desires and emotions over the well-being of their bodies unless something goes wrong.

*That each one of you know how to control his own body in holiness and honor (1 Thessalonians 4:4).*

The physical health of our bodies definitely plays a significant role in our overall mental, emotional, and spiritual health.

Taking care of the bodies God has given us is good stewardship; it affects our entire lives.

*You are not your own, for you were bought with a price. So glorify God in your body (1 Corinthians 6:20).*

Again, I say: "You are not your own, it's just on loan."

Spiritual health is a priority; however, our physical health also plays a vital role in growth, ministry, and our all-around productivity.

Everything we do in the body matters to God: how we eat, what we do, and our emotions; there is no separation of responsibilities when taking care of what we house the Holy Spirit in.

As we covered in the previous chapter, to sanctify is to set apart for God, to take care of something for a set function or purpose.

Peter encourages us in the next verse to remain holy and set apart as He, Jesus was set apart.

> *But as he who called you is holy, you also be holy in all your conduct, since it is written, "You shall be holy, for I am holy"*
> *(1 Peter 1:15-16).*

We are to be holy in our conduct, but what do we need to do to achieve this?

To sanctify your body for God, you need to take care of it. It is a great responsibility to take care of something God values and has placed in your care.

Through God's Word, we are told how to take care of the bodies God has fashioned for us.

You are not your own; you are God's, bought with the blood of Christ and housing the Holy Spirit.

The Word of God addresses six areas, which have direct instructions on how we sanctify and take care of our bodies:

1. Treat the body right
2. Eating right
3. Exercise
4. Sleep
5. Rest
6. Mental & Emotional health

- ***Treat the body right***

The aim is to keep the body free from sin, all kinds of infections and free from abuse.

Many times, when we think of those who abuse their bodies, we consider things like cutting one's self or self-harming through drugs or alcohol. But there are more common, widely accepted practices, which abuse or fail to take care of our bodies in today's society.

*Flee from sexual immorality. Every other sin a person commits is outside the body, but the sexually immoral person sins against his own body*
*(1 Corinthians 6:18).*

You are in control of what you do to your body. If you control yourself and walk in the spirit, you can control the actions of your body.

> *But I say, walk by the Spirit, and you will not gratify*
> *the desires of the flesh*
> *(Galatians 5:16).*

The way we should treat our bodies is rarely taught or shared amongst each other in conversations. We often leave it to the individual to have the good sense not to harm or abuse the body.

The truth is many people only discuss the treatment of the body when they are trying to prevent an unexpected abusive situation. We live is a society where sexual immorality is acceptable and discussion of how we should treat the body is only done in some circles.

However, in some instances, we are given guidelines on how we should treat our flesh. On the other hand, sometimes, we are not warned, and it requires the use of wisdom as our guide.

For example, piercings are mentioned in the Bible but never to prohibit the practice. Where there is no clear yes or no, wisdom is required so that you do not go to the extreme and turn your body into a human pin cushion.

Remember, whatever you do, it should be done for God's glory, not your own.

> *So, whether you eat or drink, or whatever you do, do*
> *all to the glory of God*
> *(1 Corinthians 10:31).*

There are other scriptures, which are more direct about how we should treat our bodies and the consequences of doing them harm.

> *You shall not make any cuts on your body for the dead*
> *or tattoo yourselves: I am the LORD*
> *(Leviticus 19:28).*

> *You are the sons of the LORD your God. You shall not*
> *cut yourselves or make any baldness on your*
> *foreheads for the dead*
> *(Deuteronomy 14:1).*

> *Let marriage be held in honor among all, and let the*
> *marriage bed be undefiled, for God will judge the*
> *sexually immoral and adulterous*
> *(Hebrews 13:4).*

In society, sex outside of marriage is commonplace and to a lesser degree, infidelity in marriage is championed where society sees a justifiable reason—often when observed in films and TV shows.

Like with all studies of the Word of God, it's good to know when the Word of God is giving direct or indirect advice and if the time the word was given must be taken into context.

However, what you should not do is ignore the Word or dismiss it for your own purposes.

*The body is not meant for sexual immorality, but for the Lord, and the Lord for the body*
*(1 Corinthians 6:13).*

Your body is meant for the Lord and the Lord is for the body. Consider what you are doing to your body and whether it glorifies God or yourself.

*Whatever you do, work heartily, as for the Lord and not for men*
*(Colossians 3:23).*

- **Eating right**

According to experts, many diseases are preventable through proper nutrition and exercise.

To consider or suggest food and good health are not priorities is to suggest that God isn't concerned about health. However, we know He is as Jesus dedicated so much time to making people well and restoring their health.

How you control your appetite will affect every area of your life. When we accept or sanction food addictions as acceptable, we open the door for other addictions and indisciplines. What we eat and how we eat affect our spiritual lives just as they do the physical.

Esau sold his birthright for a bowl of stew because his appetite controlled his judgment. Many people forfeit certain spiritual blessings simply because they can't say no to food or the wrong foods.

What you put into your body is very important to God. It determines your health, feeds you nutrients and sustains your life.

We are advised in the Word of God not to abuse our bodies when it comes to food and drink. This ranges from under eating to over eating and drinking.

We put things into our bodies that contribute to their abuse and harm. Equally so are the loads of food we fail to eat, which can bring about healing and good health.

A recent research by the California Institute said that over 80% of the sicknesses we have in our bodies derive from what we do with our bodies. Sixty–eight percent of the sicknesses are caused by our failure eat the right foods that produce the nutrients required to maintain our natural health and vitality.

While I do not seek to promote any particular diet in this book, I will say that we need to start putting more natural foods and fewer substitutes and processed foods into our bodies.

The natural and whole foods come packed with the nutrients and proteins our bodies need to stay in their God- given natural states.

Nowadays, it is not hard to search the internet or watch TV ads to find good advice on eating healthy foods that benefit our bodies.

The foods you eat and when you eat should be done to glorify God. You cannot eat something harmful to your body for the pleasure it gives you if it is also damaging the body at the same time.

*So, whether you eat or drink, or whatever you do, do all to the glory of God (1 Corinthians 10:31).*

No two people will maintain the same diet. Something that agrees with you may not agree with someone else. For example, foods a diabetic should avoid can be consumed by another person without discrimination. Seek guidance and wisdom for what you need.

We are also advised against overindulgence, which is hard to do in a society that focuses on food pleasures and treats.

*If you have found honey, eat only enough for you, lest you have your fill of it and vomit it (Proverbs 25:16).*

You must remember that food is to sustain you and should not be abused. Nothing stops you from enjoying your meal as long as you do not abuse that pleasure.

> *Food is meant for the stomach and the stomach for
> food—and God will destroy both one and the other
> (1 Corinthians 6:13).*

Don't make food your idol; it'll pass away. It's only for this life.

God is so protective of how you treat your body that in the book of Proverbs, you will find the most shocking example used to encourage you to get your eating under control.

> *And put a knife to your throat if you are given to
> appetite
> (Proverbs 23:2).*

To read more about the power of food and the role it plays in our spiritual lives, growth, and ministries, I suggest you read my book *Food for Thought – The Anointing of Discipline.*

- **Exercise**

Exercise is vital to the body. In the western world, we have created so many conveniences that we can easily neglect the basic things the body needs to be healthy; for example, walking. Movements that the body would normally make as part of its day to day functions have been removed because of our societies' advancement in industry and technology. However, this does not mean we are to stop or reduce our God-given movements.

You may not be a gym person, but everyone can keep the body moving at home, in parks, and in community halls. Get off the bus or train at an earlier stop to walk. Turn domestic chores into workout sessions—just a few ideas.

Exercise is well-known for relieving depression, providing a positive boost to the mood and offering great aid to psychological conditions. It also improves one's self-esteem and self-confidence.

The reason for this is that exercising your body releases chemicals called endorphins, which reduce the brain's perception of pain. This chemical also triggers a positive in the body similar to morphine, without the addiction or dependency attached to morphine—thankfully.

Regular exercise has also been proven to reduce stress and improve sleep. I will discuss emotions like stress and sleep further in the book.

> *Beloved, I pray that all may go well with you and that*
> *you may be in good health, as it goes well with your*
> *soul*
> *(3 John 1:2).*

The soul signifies the mind, emotion, and will. God wants your entire body to be healthy as well as your soul.

*An athlete is not crowned unless he competes*
*according to the rules*
*(2 Timothy 2:5).*

Exercise does not have to be rigorous but it should be diligent and constant. Occasional exercise spread out between long periods like weeks or month often accomplishes very little to nothing.

Also, be careful not to fall into the trap of exercising to burn the calories obtained from constant and regular bad eating. Unhealthy food will still harm the body. Even if the exercise reduces the weight visually, it will not remove the damage.

*Every athlete exercises self-control in all things. They*
*do it to receive a perishable wreath, but we an*
*imperishable But I discipline my body and keep it*
*under control, lest after preaching to others I myself*
*should be disqualified*
*(1 Corinthians 9:25-27).*

Start taking the healthy advice you often hear about and offer it to others and your children.

*For while bodily training is of some value*
*(1 Timothy 4:8).*

Remember, exercise has value even in small consistent amounts.

- **Sleep**

  *It is in vain that you rise up early and go late to rest, eating the bread of anxious toil; for he gives to his beloved sleep*
  *(Psalm 127:2).*

Sleep is very important to your good health and well-being. Getting quality sleep can help protect your mental health, physical health, quality of life, and safety.

Sleep deficiency can cause instant damage to your body or it can create long-lasting problems over time. Lack of sleep or not enough sleep can affect the way you think, react, work or learn. It can also contribute to some chronic health problems.

I was watching a movie where the hero was asked if he needed to sleep. He replied: "Sleep is overrated – I'll sleep when I'm dead." He then loaded his gun and continued his pursuit of the bad guys. A good pursuit does not justify lack of sleep.

Most of us live in cities that never sleep. There are round-the-clock shops with rota jobs to cover every hour within a 24-hour day. Moreover, our lives are so busy that we try to cram as much into it at the expense of shorter sleeping hours.

Even our TVs remain on for 24 hours so we can get entertainment anytime of the day. There is 24-hour stimulation on demand.

I once heard that the West had the most sleep deprived countries in the world. This is not a fact to be proud of.

In looking after these God-created, fashioned and beautifully designed bodies, we must not forget the importance of sleep.

Shutting down the body in the state of sleep is extremely beneficial for your well-being. Here are just a few advantages of doing so over 7 hours.

*Below is a list taken from NYU online sleep study*
*https://www.nyu.edu/life/safety-health-wellness/live-well-nyu/priority-areas/sleep.html*

1. Improved memory - NYU Langone Medical Center has shown that sleep helps you learn better whether it is a new language or a sporting skill.

2. Research has shown that sleep adds years to your life. A 2010 study of women aged 50 – 79 showed that more deaths occurred in those who had less than five hours sleep each night.

3. Reduces inflammation – inflammation is linked to heart disease, strokes, diabetes, and arthritis. Research has shown that getting less than 6 hours sleep a night leaves you with higher blood levels of inflammatory protein.

4. Known to contribute to ADHD in kids who do not get enough sleep.

5. Aids tremendously with a healthy weight balance and prompting any weight loss diet you may be on. You will also be able to build muscle more easily.

6. You'll be happier, have better moods and fewer problems with depression, low self-esteem and anxiety according to the "Business insider UK Lifestyle" online research into sleep.

*If you lie down, you will not be afraid; when you lie down, your sleep will be sweet*
*(Proverbs 3:24).*

There are over 25 health benefits that can be easily found online, which support and promote getting a good night's sleep.

God, who made these bodies instructed us to rest as this is one of the blessings to the body, which houses the Holy Spirit. Remember, your body is not your own, it's God's, and you are the steward of it.

Like everything that can be done to the body, sleep can also be abused; sleep is meant for you to rest each day so your body can be restored to continue its functions effectively. You should not indulge in sleeping beyond reason.

- **Rest**

*Come to me, all you who are weary and burdened,*
*and I will give you rest*
*(Matthews 11: 28).*

One of the hardest things for us to do in today's society is to rest. This is not the same as sleep, although sleep is rest. The rest I am talking about is where you take a conscious break from work. It is about taking the time to pamper yourself, play golf, fellowship with God,lounge and maybe socialise with others as well as relaxing—taking a day of rest.

Although it is good to have intermittent breaks during the day so we do not get burned out, the rest we are encouraged to take is a full day for oneself. Many people believe a day of rest or the Sabbath as it is called in the Bible, was a day given to the Hebrews only in the Ten Commandments.

*Remember the sabbath day, to keep it holy. Six days shalt thou labour, and do all thy work: But the seventh day is the sabbath of the LORD thy God: in it thou shalt not do any work, thou, nor thy son, nor thy daughter, thy manservant, nor thy maidservant, nor thy cattle, nor thy stranger that is within thy gates: For in six days the LORD made heaven and earth, the sea, and all that in them is, and rested the seventh day: wherefore the LORD blessed the sabbath day, and hallowed it (Exodus 20:11).*

An important note from this passage of scripture is that it starts with the word "remember." This was not something newly introduced to the Hebrews; it was something already established in the beginning.

The passage goes on to say that a day of rest was given in the beginning. That means, it was not just for a set of people, God's people, but it was for everyone on earth to have a day of rest from their labour.

*So God blessed the seventh day and made it holy because on it God rested from all his work that he had done in creation*

*(Genesis 2:3).*

The Sabbath is also related to a day of worship; however, for the sake of the physical body, we are focusing on its importance for our rest.

The word "Sabbath" in the Hebrew verb is called *Shabbbat* and means "to rest from labor."

You may feel that you can either take it or leave it. However, for the Christian, this is a very important part of our relationship with God.

> *You are to speak to the people of Israel and say, 'Above all you shall keep my Sabbaths, for this is a sign between me and you throughout your generations, that you may know that I, the LORD, sanctify you*
> *(Exodus 31:13).*

It is important to differentiate between rest as in sleep and a day of rest. A lot of people feel they get rest every day as they see sleeping or the wind down a few hours before bedtime as their rest period. But stopping for a few hours is not the same as intentionally taking time like a full day to rest the body.

One of the main reasons we do not rest is because we see our work as our worth. The more I do, the more I get, the more worthy I become. People see value in what they do. The more they can fit in and accomplish, the more they feel they have achieved.

This is particularly seen in the church where those in ministry fill their days with activities and functions. For example, you seldom hear of pastors who do not have something in their diaries to do every day.

This, however, should not be the case; our worth was made clear by God, Jesus, and the Holy Spirit way before we engaged in work.

> *Then, because so many people were coming and going*
> *that they did not even have chance to eat, he said to*
> *then " Come with me by  yourselves to a quiet place*
> *and get some rest"*
> *(Mark 6:31).*

Jesus saw the need for the disciples and Him to retreat and rest. Often times, this happened while the crowd was still requiring more teachings and miracles from Him. Who today would stop a revival to get a day of rest? "I'll rest when it's over" would be the reply.

Doing housework and chores cannot be considered as taking a day of rest either. A lot of people take a day on the weekend to rest from their workplaces. However, they engage in a different kind of work—housework. Doing housework instead of office work is not resting the body. Remember not to lose sight that the purpose of a day of rest is to take care of the body.

There are many reasons and drivers, which cause us to forsake rest; one of them is discontentment. The pursuit to gain or do more so that you can increase your worth needs to be replaced with the spirit and feeling of contentment as a starting point.

*For the love of money is a root of all kinds of evil.*
*Some people eager for money, have wandered from*
*the faith and pierced themselves with many griefs*
*(1 Timothy 6:10).*

The scripture you have just read is a well-known scripture, but it is rarely quoted in full. People tend to stop at "root of all evil."

However, it's important to note, the real warning given here is that the pursuit of money leads many away from the faith.

We work on rest day       s, volunteer overtime, work long hours on projects and make plans to gain more money or become rich but at what cost?

As we have seen, rest is ordained by God, and it is a requirement of our faith rather than an option. Therefore, are we not drawn away from vital parts of our faith by our pursuit of money?

Note, the scripture does not say as long as the motives are noble then the pursuit of more money is noble—the focus is on what you give up to pursue it—being drawn away from the faith.

One way of freeing yourself for a day of rest is being free to say "no."

> *An impulsive vow is a trap; later you'll wish you could*
> *get out of it*
> *(Proverbs 20:25 MSG).*

How many times have we said yes to our kids, families or friends without considering the odds or time required to deliver?

I have seen people overly embrace a common head cold to avoid doing what they had promised or going somewhere they had committed to be but now want out.

Don't be eager to volunteer or offer your time until you consider the cost. Good intentions without actions are planned disappointments.

> *Even youths shall faint and be weary, and young men*
> *shall fall exhausted; but they who wait for the* Lord
> *shall renew their strength; they shall mount up with*
> *wings like eagles; they shall run and not be weary;*
> *they shall walk and not faint*
> *(Isaiah 40:30-31).*

It pays to rest in the Lord for it is in Him that a day of rest can refuel you like a week long holiday.

We all have things to do; we cannot escape some kind of work or toil, but we can build rest days into our lives to regenerate the body, soul, and spirit. In doing so, you will accomplish so much more than you would have if you did not take a break.

I have often heard it said that there is no time to rest as the Devil never takes a rest.

Your role model is Christ, not the Devil, and Christ saw the great importance of taking a rest.

*The apostles returned to Jesus and told him all that they had done and taught. And he said to them, "Come away by yourselves to a desolate place and rest a while." For many were coming and going, and they had no leisure even to eat. And they went away in the boat to a desolate (Mark 6:30-32).*

*But he would withdraw to desolate places and pray (Luke 5:16).*

*Come to me, all who labor and are heavy laden, and I will give you rest (Matthew 11:28).*

God knew that physical rest for our bodies was so important that He established it in one of the Ten Commandments.

*Observe the Sabbath day, to keep it holy. Work six days and do everything you need to do. But the*

> *seventh day is a Sabbath to GOD, your God. Don't do any work*
> *(Exodus 20:9-10).*

I mentioned earlier in the chapter that rest is not an option. The verse just read emphasises its vital requirement. Think about it, we would never say "Do not kill" was merely a suggestion made in the Ten Commandments. Yet, we do so concerning a day of rest.

The pace of life is getting faster and faster and many believe that the faster the better as you can get more accomplished. However, as often proven, the faster you go the less you accomplish.

Now, there has been much debate about which day should be used for rest. This is not new as in the apostle Paul's day, people were judged by the day they observed.

> *Therefore do not let anyone judge you by what you eat or drink, or with regard to a religious festival, a New Moon celebration or a Sabbath day*
> *(Colossians 2:16).*

The emphasis here is not letting anyone's opinion judge which day you choose to rest, but you do need a day.

*The plans of the diligent lead surely to abundance; but
everyone who is hasty comes only to poverty
( Proverbs 21:5).*

It is important to rest; you need to slow down for the good
of your body and your mental state. If you live in the fast
lane continually without resting, you will make bad
judgements or mistakes.

*Whoever makes haste with his feet misses his way
(Proverbs 19:2).*

It is important for the spirit, soul, and body that you rest.
You need to stop, reflect, recoup, and refocus.

*And he said to them, "The Sabbath was made for
man, not man for the Sabbath
(Mark 2:27).*

Jesus had to make it clear that we were not made for the
Sabbath; we were not made to sit back and do nothing.
Rather, we are all made with a purpose.

The day was made for us to take a rest from our work and
toil. Although the emphasis of rest is on a day, there is still
great value and importance in setting time aside during the
day to be still, hear God, clear your mind from stress, rest,
and relax your physical body.

> *Better is a handful of quietness than two hands of toil*
> *and a striving after wind*
> *(Ecclesiastes 4:6).*

To paraphrase Ecclesiastes 4:6, it says it is far better to have one hour of quiet time and rest than two hours of work, toil, and busying yourself chasing after things which do not last.

So is the Sabbath day of rest still relevant today? Or was it designed only for the Old Testament believers and the Jews in the New Testament? Rest, the Sabbath, is for ALL of God's people.

The day of rest is encourage to the New Testaments Christian.

> *There remains then a Sabbath-rest for the people of*
> *God, for anyone who enters Gods rest also rests from*
> *their works, just as God did from his. Let us, therefore*
> *make every effort to enter that rest so that no one will*
> *perish by following their example of disobedience*
> *(Hebrew 4:9-11).*

- o **Mental &Emotional Well-being**

> *Beloved, I pray that all may go well with you and that*
> *you may be in good health, as it goes well with your*
> *soul*

*(3 John 1:2).*

Emotional health requires having great control over your emotions and your behaviour. This comes with understanding that situations and hurdles in life are inevitable. However, we must focus on God and positive things so that we do not succumb to pressure.

There are three areas, which we need to consider when we approach mental and emotional health:

- o **Thought Patterns**
- o **Feelings**
- o **Perceptions**

**Thought Patterns**

Another thing that degenerates our mental and emotional health is what we choose to dwell on or think about. The Word of God tells us how we are to focus our thoughts.

*Finally, brothers and sisters, whatever is true, whatever is noble, whatever is right, whatever is lovely, whatever is admirable; it anything is excellent or praiseworthy, think about such things (Phillippians 4:8)*

Having a good thought pattern does not only imply a lack of mental problems; it also means your mind is able to fight against depression and many other psychological issues.

Being an emotionally healthy individual will allow you to take better care of your body and promote you to lead a productive and enjoyable life even in the face of difficult situations and circumstances.

By being emotionally healthy according to the Word, you are less likely to fall prey to depression, anxiety, and panic attacks. Emotional health also contributes to your physical wellness as emotions release chemicals into the body.

Good chemicals are released during exercise and laughter while bad or too many good chemicals are released from the brain during times of pain and stress.

*A joyful heart is good medicine, but a crushed spirit
dries up the bones
(Proverbs 17:22).*

The Word of God encourages us to think on good things as there is a mental and physical price to pay when we do not. When we walk around with un-forgiveness, anger, stress to name a few negative emotions, we cause sickness or provide negative aid to a condition within our bodies.

### Feelings

Our thought patterns heavily affect our emotions and how we feel about a thing or situation. However, there are occasions when bad feelings come upon us while we have not consciously thought about them.

How many of us have awakened feeling heavy in our spirits but have no idea why? Most of the time, we can pinpoint the source of our feelings. God cares about you as a whole and that includes your emotions; He wants to heal that area too.

*He heals the brokenhearted and binds up their wounds*
*(Psalm 147:3).*

Similar to negative thought patterns, negative feelings can damage and cause sickness to the physical body.

*Remove vexation from your heart, and put away pain from your body, for youth and the dawn of life are vanity*
*(Ecclesiastes 11:10).*

*A tranquil heart gives life to the flesh, but envy makes the bones rot*
*(Proverbs 14:30).*

Although the scriptures do not use chemical terms like endorphins from the brain, the message is quite clear—how we feel, our emotions can have a damaging effect on our bodies healthwise.

Therefore, we are encouraged to focus on good and God things for the body's well-being, our thoughts, and reactions.

Our words spoken bring destruction or health to our bodies.

> *Gracious words are like a honeycomb, sweetness to the soul and health to the body*
> *(Proverbs 16:24).*

God is there and He's waiting to take our burdens and issues upon Himself.

## Perception

This area is one of the most destructive when it comes to attacks on our mental and emotional health. There are two definitions of the word "perception":

*1 -The ability to see, hear or become aware of something through the senses.*

*2 - The way in which something is regarded, understood or interpreted*

I wish to focus on the second translation: The ability to understand or interpret something. Attempts to understand and interpret something with only half of the information can be detrimental. Many worries, anxieties, anger, and frustrations tend to be based on the individual's perception and understanding. This leads to expectations and sleepless nights worrying about something, which may never happen or reacting to what they expect rather than what is.

God tells us to bring all our issues to Him so that He can deal with them. We can rest easy due to His help and intervention in our situations and circumstances.

> *Do not be anxious about anything, but in everything by prayer and supplication with thanksgiving let your requests be made known to God. And the peace of God, which surpasses all understanding, will guard your hearts and your minds in Christ Jesus (Philippians 4:6-7).*

It does not matter if you perceive the situation wrongly; take your cares and concerns to God as a first point.  How many of us have worried about something that never happened or have been worked up for an argument, which did not take place?

> *Casting all your anxieties on him, because he cares for you (1 Peter 5:7).*

Cast your cares on Him. God has a way of bringing you through all situations.

> *When the righteous cry for help, the LORD hears and delivers them out of all their troubles. The LORD is near to the brokenhearted and saves the crushed in spirit. Many are the afflictions of the righteous, but the LORD delivers him out of them all. He keeps all his bones; not one of them is broken*
> *(Psalm 34:17-20).*

We tend to worry about the future, what will happen, what we have seen before or are expecting. When these thoughts are negative, they tend to make us anxious. God has told us the dangers of worrying and how it accomplishes and changes nothing.

> *Therefore I tell you, do not be anxious about your life, what you will eat or what you will drink, nor about your body, what you will put on. Is not life more than food, and the body more than clothing? Look at the birds of the air: they neither sow nor reap nor gather into barns, and yet your heavenly Father feeds them. Are you not of more value than they? And which of you by being anxious can add a single hour to his span of life? And why are you anxious about clothing? Consider the lilies of the field, how they grow: they neither toil nor spin, yet I tell you, even Solomon in all his glory was not arrayed like one of these*
> *(Matthew 6:25 – 29).*

God has already planned a solution or a way to be free from anything that will stress you or cause you emotional and mental pressure:

*No temptation has overtaken you that is not common to man. God is faithful, and he will not let you be tempted beyond your ability, but with the temptation he will also provide the way of escape, that you may be able to endure it*
*(1Corinthians 10:13).*

We are encouraged that in the constant pursuit of God, we tend to worry less. So in times of worry and anxiety, we are to seek God and His way of doing things (the kingdom of God).

There is too much to contend with on a single day for us to try fixing tomorrow.

*But seek first the kingdom of God and his righteousness, and all these things will be added to you. "Therefore do not be anxious about tomorrow, for tomorrow will be anxious for itself. Sufficient for the day is its own trouble*
*(Matthew 6:33 – 34).*

God wants you free from anxiety; it is heavy on the heart and destroys the body.

> *Anxiety in a man's heart weighs him down, but a good word makes him glad*
> *(Proverbs 12:2).*

Mental health plays a major role in our lives; it affects us all directly or indirectly. We cannot avoid it. God has put so much in His Word to encourage us to think and feel differently. With a renewed mindset, we become better physically, spiritually, and mentally. We would be unwise to ignore His instructions.

> *I can do all things through Christ who strengthens me*
> *(Philippians 4:13).*

> *And my God will supply every need of yours according to his riches in glory in Christ Jesus*
> *(Philippians 4:19).*

> *For nothing will be impossible with God*
> *(Luke 1:37).*

Perhaps, you are saying that it's not that easy to let go of certain issues or things that frustrate or annoy you; maybe you just can't forgive or holding hate in your heart. The preceding scriptures tell us, how these feelings damage your body.

However it is possible if you do not face these emotions alone. Trust God with your concerns; you are in safe hands.

*The fear of man lays a snare, but whoever trusts in the*
*L*ORD *is safe*
*(Proverbs 29:25).*

*Trust in the* L*ORD* *with all your heart, and do not lean*
*on your own understanding. In all your ways*
*acknowledge him, and he will make straight your*
*paths*
*(Proverbs 3:5-6).*

## Chapter 5: Consequences of Not Taking Care of the Body

At this point, I hope you have gained some insight of how you are currently treating your body, the successes, and pitfalls you may already be experiencing and how you can improve in areas of health.

However, you may be thinking, these are good points and nice suggestions but you are too set in your ways or cannot be bothered to make the changes this late in your life.

Firstly, let me say that it is never too late for change; it does not matter what your age or where you are in your life. You can always make changes.

Secondly, taking care of our physical body is a requirement not a suggestion.

> *Do you not know that you are God's temple and that God's Spirit dwells in you? If anyone destroys God's temple, God will destroy him. For God's temple is holy, and you are that temple*
> *(1Corinthians 3:16 – 17).*

In the above scripture, we read that we are accountable directly or indirectly for how we treat our bodies.

This means that once we are saved and the Holy Spirit takes up residence, we have the responsibility for the maintenance and proper treatment of the house (temple) He occupies.

Equally, people who choose to abuse your body through misadventure, physical assaults, mental & verbal assaults or by your own permission are also held accountable.

*Or do you not know that your body is a temple of the Holy Spirit within you, whom you have from God? You are not your own, for you were bought with a price. So glorify God in your body*
*(1 Corinthians 6: 19- 20).*

Whatever you do in your body should be to glorify God. You need to ask: "How would God consider this treatment of my body?"

*Now may the God of peace himself sanctify you completely, and may your whole spirit and soul and body be kept blameless at the coming of our Lord Jesus Christ. He who calls you is faithful; he will surely do it*
*(1 Thessalonians 5:23-24).*

God wants all of us to be blameless before Him. That's why He includes our bodies in the above verse. Moreover, in the next scripture, He urges that we keep our bodies from defilement.

> *Since we have these promises, beloved, let us cleanse*
> *ourselves from every defilement of body and spirit,*
> *bringing holiness to completion in the fear of God*
> *(2 Corinthians 7:1).*

Remember, you have the authority in this body to make a change. The following scripture confirms that you control your body:

> *For this is the will of God, your sanctification: that you*
> *abstain from sexual immorality; that each one of you*
> *know how to control his own body in holiness and*
> *honor, not in the passion of lust like the Gentiles who*
> *do not know God*
> *(1 Thessalonians 4:3-5).*

There are many sicknesses, relationships, and states of mind, which can be reversed but many people prefer to live with them.

We would be unwise if we have the opportunity to repair our bodies by following and acting in accordance with God's Word but we reject it. Rather, we should apply it to our lives for the sanctification and care of our bodies.

You may be at a place where you have mistreated your body so long that it's hard to change or there are now strongholds of addictions, which need to be broken before you can get the repairs underway.

*For we do not have a high priest who is unable to sympathize with our weaknesses, but one who in every respect has been tempted as we are, yet without sin. Let us then with confidence draw near to the throne of grace, that we may receive mercy and find grace to help in times of need*
*(Hebrews 4:15-16).*

God understands everything you are going through— the temptations and the trials.  He cared enough to send His Son so that He could be touched by our feelings and struggles.

Nothing is too small—from food addictions to physical attacks—He cares about you and what happens to and in your body.

*No temptation has overtaken you that is not common to man. God is faithful, and he will not let you be tempted beyond your ability, but with the temptation he will also provide the way of escape, that you may be able to endure it*
*(1 Corinthians 10:13).*

God knows how much you can take and if He says you can fight a temptation or an urge, He says it because He knows it. He has also planned the way of escape from the temptation or stronghold holding you—that's how He can tell us to resist.

> *Let no one say when he is tempted, "I am being tempted by God," for God cannot be tempted with evil, and he himself tempts no one. But each person is tempted when he is lured and enticed by his own desire*
> *(James 1:13-14).*

I have heard people say God made them go through some sort of bodily abuse like drugs, drinking alcohol or assault so they can be well placed to minister to others.

God will use you and whatever you have to bring to His table, but He does not equip you with bodily issues to build His kingdom.

If you are embracing sickness in your body, for example, you may be thinking God is glorified somehow; it is time to change your mindset. He is glorified in your deliverance from the sickness and what you do through sickness – not the sickness itself.

In the book of John Chapter 9, we read of a blind man Jesus healed. This man was blind from birth; he neither asked or cried out for healing nor did he express concerns about his condition. Yet, in healing him, Jesus expressed that the benefit of this man's condition was in the glory of his deliverance.

The freedom you have been given in your body is in Christ, not freedom to the world to do as you did before:

> *For freedom Christ has set us free stand firm therefore and so not submit again to a yoke of slavery (Galatians 5:2).*

You have been given divine power to break the strongholds over your life.  Use it!

> *For though we walk in the flesh, we are not waging war according to the flesh. For the weapons of our warfare are not of the flesh but have divine power to destroy strongholds. We destroy arguments and every lofty opinion raised against the knowledge of God, and take every thought captive to obey Christ (2 Corinthians 10:3-5).*

## Chapter 6: Change for the Better

*Jesus Christ is the same yesterday and today and
forever
(Hebrews 13:8).*

In a changing world, it's good to know that God and His Word never changes. Why is this so important and good news? because in a constantly changing world, there is a presumption that everything changes—including the Word.

I have spoken to people who believe that bodily healing was for a particular dispensation of time, which has passed. Speaking in tongues has almost been eradicated in some churches and repentance is rarely mentioned when encouraging new believers to accept Jesus as their Lord and Savior.

I raise these points not to go into theological teaching, but to emphasise that the Word of God is unchanging even if people choose to pick and change it over the years.

Therefore, if the Word says God will support you through your changes for the better, you should trust that He will do it.

*Sanctify them in the truth; your word is truth
(John 17:17).*

*All Scripture is breathed out by God and profitable for teaching, for reproof, for correction, and for training in righteousness, that the man of God may be competent, equipped for every good work*
*(2 Timothy 3 16-17).*

*When the Spirit of truth comes, he will guide you into all the truth, for he will not speak on his own authority, but whatever he hears he will speak, and he will declare to you the things that are to come*
*(John 16:13).*

*Knowing this first of all, that no prophecy of Scripture comes from someone's own interpretation. For no prophecy was ever produced by the will of man, but men spoke from God as they were carried along by the Holy Spirit*
*(2 Peter 1:20-21).*

Focus on your change with help from an unchanging God. It is time to assess how you have treated your body in the six areas mentioned in Chapter 4.

*Have I not commanded you? Be strong and courageous. Do not be frightened, and do not be dismayed, for the LORD your God is with you wherever you go*
*(Joshua 1:9).*

By allowing God through is Word to change those areas in your life, you can rest assured that any direction in which He takes you is the best direction for you.

> *For I know the plans I have for you, declares the L*ORD*,*
> *plans for welfare and not for evil, to give you a future*
> *and a hope*
> *(Jeremiah 29:11).*

Once you have identified the areas for change, the next step is simple: take it to God in prayer.  This sounds so easy but strangely, I find people tend to talk or complain about their health, weight, relationships, stress, and emotional issues more than they pray about them.

> *Do not be anxious about anything, but in everything*
> *by prayer and supplication with thanksgiving let your*
> *requests be made known to God. And the peace of*
> *God, which surpasses all understanding, will guard*
> *your hearts and your minds in Christ Jesus*
> *(Philippians 4:6-7).*

When praying, I always encourage the prayer for wisdom and knowledge.

> *An intelligent heart acquires knowledge, and the ear*
> *of the wise seeks knowledge*
> *(Proverbs 18:15).*

*Desire without knowledge is not good, and whoever
makes haste with his feet misses his way
(Proverbs 19:2).*

Years ago, I was rushed to the hospital because I was faint
and could not walk straight. As I had given birth just a week
prior to the fainting spell, I was rushed through A&E and
given attention straight away. I was told by a doctor that I
was anemic and that I needed to have a transfusion by the
end of the day or I may not make it to the end of the week.

This was a lot of information for me to absorb in one
afternoon, and while I was still processing it, a nurse had
stuck an IV connection into my hand awaiting my consent
for the transfusion to take place within the hour.

In my panic and fear, I kept saying no, and much to my
husband and doctor's disappointment, they let me leave
but told me to come back before the end of the week.

As the wheelchair took me to the car, I remember saying to
God: "Lord tell me what I need to do to put this right."

The next day, when the midwife came to check my
daughter and me, I mentioned what happened the day
before. She looked at me, smiled, wrote the name of a high
iron tonic drink sold in most shops and told my husband to
purchase it.

He swiftly left the house and purchased as much as he could afford that day.

Four days later, I went back to the doctors and the result the following week said my blood showed significant improvement. The doctor not only said I no longer needed the transfusion, but he questioned the original blood reading as improvement should not have occurred that quickly without a transfusion.

This is a clear case of knowledge helping to bring about a change.  Sometimes, we seek miracles to create change but God has provided so much we can do with wisdom and knowledge. Many things that attack the body can easily be changed or fixed with more knowledge and wisdom.

I truly believe God sent the midwife in answer to my prayers; He has promised the same to us all who ask Him.

*God is not man, that he should lie, or a son of man, that he should change his mind. Has he said, and will he not do it? Or has he spoken, and will he not fulfill it?*
*(Numbers 23:19).*

You may have tried to change before. Maybe, you started to exercise and tried to get more rest, but it all ended without any real results. Don't worry about what happened before; every hour offers us an opportunity to start afresh.

*Remember not the former things, nor consider the
things of old. Behold, I am doing a new thing; now it
springs forth, do you not perceive it? I will make a way
in the wilderness and rivers in the desert
(Isaiah 43:18-19).*

It is not too late to start to change and take care of your body for the better and the glory of God.

*May the God of hope fill you with all joy and peace in
believing, so that by the power of the Holy Spirit you
may abound in hope
(Romans 15:13).*

# <u>Prayer</u>

Dear heavenly Father, I thank You for making this body according to Psalm 139:14. I accept that I am fearfully and wonderfully made.

I thank You Father God for making me; I thank You, Jesus, for saving me, and I thank You Holy Spirit for Your indwelling in my life.

I ask You for forgiveness for the times and areas of my life that I have not submitted to You and taken care of my body.

Father, I ask You for the wisdom to show me how to act right, eat right, exercise right, go to bed on time, rest right and think right. You tell me in Proverbs 4:7 to get wisdom and understanding. So I ask You according to James 1:5 for more wisdom so I know what I need to do to honor You more with my body.

Father God, I give to You honor and consider You in all that I do. I thank You that I am wonderfully made and blessed in this body by You and for Your service.

Amen.

## Notes

71